Advice to Little Girls

Text & design © 2014 Engage Books
Illustrations © 2014 Anna Shukeylo
Compilation © 2014 A.R. Roumanis

All rights reserved. No part of this book may be stored in a retrieval system, reproduced or transmitted in any form or by any other means without written permission from the publisher or a licence from the Canadian Copyright Licensing Agency. Critics and reviewers may quote brief passages in connection with a review or critical article in any media.

Every reasonable effort has been made to contact the copyright holders of all material reproduced in this book.

 ENGAGE BOOKS

Mailing address
PO BOX 4608
Main Station Terminal
349 West Georgia Street
Vancouver, BC
Canada, V6B 4A1

www.engagebooks.ca

Edited & compiled by: A.R. Roumanis
Illustrated by: Anna Shukeylo
Designed by: A.R. Roumanis

FIRST EDITION / FIRST PRINTING

LIBRARY AND ARCHIVES CANADA CATALOGUING IN PUBLICATION

Twain, Mark, 1835–1910, author
    Advice to little girls / by Mark Twain ; illustrated by Anna Shukeylo.

Issued in print and electronic formats.
ISBN 978-1-77226-016-8 (pbk.). –
ISBN 978-1-77226-017-5 (bound). –
ISBN 978-1-77226-020-5 (pdf). –
ISBN 978-1-77226-018-2 (epub). –
ISBN 978-1-77226-019-9 (kindle)

1. Girls – Conduct of life – Juvenile humor.
I. Shukeylo, Anna, 1988–, illustrator
II. Title.

PZ7.T89AD 2014   J818'.402   C2014-906006-8
                                                      C2014-906007-6

"Only one thing, is impossible for God:
to find any sense in any copyright law on the planet."
mark twain

Advice to Little Girls

By Mark Twain

EDITED & COMPILED BY A.R. ROUMANIS
ILLUSTRATED BY ANNA SHUKEYLO

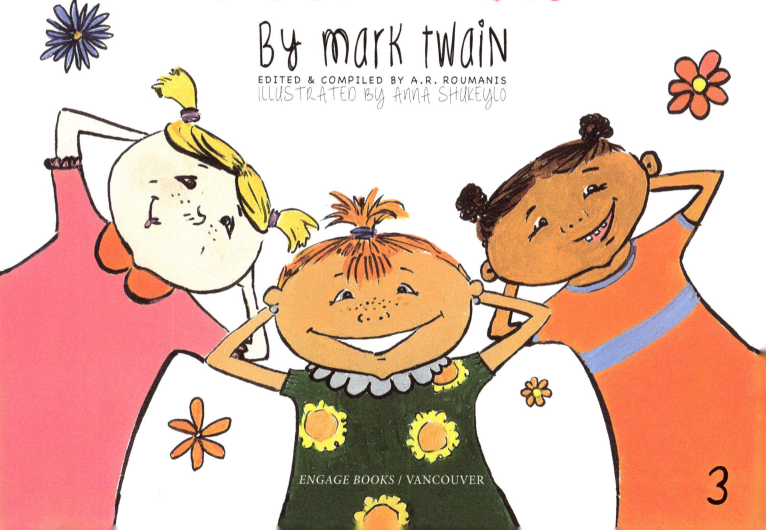

ENGAGE BOOKS / VANCOUVER

Good little girls ought not to make mouths at their teachers for every **trifling*** offense. This retaliation should only be resorted to under **peculiarly** aggravated circumstances.

*What does that mean?
See page 27 for definitions of bolded words.

Always respect your superiors;

if you have any.

If you have nothing but a rag-doll stuffed with sawdust,
while one of your more fortunate little playmates has a costly China one,
you should treat her with a show of kindness nevertheless.

And you ought not to attempt
to make a forcible swap with her
unless your **conscience** would justify you in it,
and you know you are able to do it.

You ought never to take your little brother's
"chewing-gum" away from him by main force;
it is better to rope him in with the promise
of the first two dollars and a half you find
floating down the river on a **grindstone**.
In the artless simplicity natural to this time of life,
he will regard it as a perfectly fair transaction.
In all ages of the world this **eminently plausible** fiction
has lured the **obtuse** infant to financial ruin and disaster.

It's no wonder that truth is stranger than fiction.

Fiction has to make sense.

If at any time you find it necessary
to correct your brother,
do not correct him with mud –
never, on any account, throw mud at him,
because it will spoil his clothes.
It is better to **scald** him a little,
for then you obtain desirable results.
You secure his immediate attention
to the lessons you are **inculcating**,
and at the same time
your hot water will have a tendency
to move **impurities** from his person,
and possibly the skin, in spots.

Anger is an acid

that can do more harm

to the **vessel** in which it is stored

than to anything on which it is poured.

If your mother tells you to do a thing,
it is wrong to reply that you won't.
It is better and more becoming to **intimate**
that you will do as she bids you,
and then afterward act quietly
in the matter according to the **dictates**
of your best judgment.

Always obey your parents when they are present.

You should ever bear in mind
that it is to your kind parents
that you are **indebted** for your food,
and for the privilege of staying home from school
when you let on that you are sick.

Therefore you ought to respect their little prejudices,

and humor their little whims,

and put up with their little **foibles**

until they get to crowding you too much.

Good little girls always show marked **deference** for the aged. You ought never to "**sass**" old people unless they "sass" you first.

Age is an issue of mind over matter.

If you don't mind, it doesn't matter.

Noise proves nothing.

Often a hen who has merely laid an egg cackles as if she had laid an **asteroid**.

Better to keep your mouth shut and appear stupid than to open it and remove all doubt.

We should be careful to get out of an experience
only the wisdom that is in it – and stop there,
lest we be like the cat that sits down on a hot stovelid.

She will never sit down on a hot stove-lid again –

and that is well;

but also she will never sit down on a cold one anymore.

Twenty years from now
you will be more disappointed
by the things that you didn't do
than by the ones you did do.

So throw off the **bowlines**.

Sail away from the safe harbor.

Catch the **trade winds** in your sails.

Explore. Dream. Discover.

Advice to Little Girls

Activity

What would be your best advice to give to little girls? In the space provided, write down your advice to little girls. Draw a picture to go along with your advice.

Advice to Little Girls

QUIZ

1 What is truth stranger than?

2 Why should you not throw mud at your little brother?

3 Age is an issue of mind over...?

4 What does a cackling hen believe it has laid?

5 What did the cat sit on?

6 In twenty years, what will you be most disappointed with?

Answers:
1. Fiction
2. It will spoil his clothes
3. Matter
4. An Asteroid
5. A hot stoild
6. The things you didn't do

what does that mean?

asteroid: a small rocky body in outer space
bowlines: a rope used to keep the edge of a sail pulled forward
conscience: a person's sense of right and wrong
deference: polite submission and respect
dictates: to speak or act in an authoritative way
eminently: to a great degree
foibles: a minor weakness in someone's character
grindstone: a thick disc of stone used to sharpen or polish metal tools
impurities: unwanted substances that are found in something else
inculcating: to teach an attitude, idea, or habit to someone
indebted: owing gratitude for a service or favor
intimate: to say or suggest something in an indirect way
obtuse: slow to understand
peculiarly: in an unusual, or odd way
plausible: worthy of being accepted as reasonable
sass: to be cheeky or rude to someone
scald: to injure with very hot liquid or steam
trade winds: wind blowing towards the equator
trifling: something of very little importance
vessel: a container used to store liquid or small objects

ENGAGE WITH OUR BOOKS ON YOUR MOBILE OR TABLET
WWW.ENGAGEBOOKS.CA

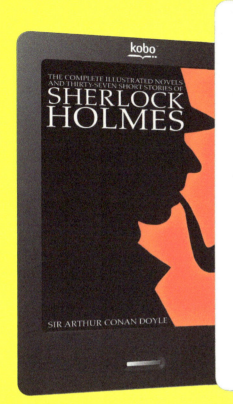
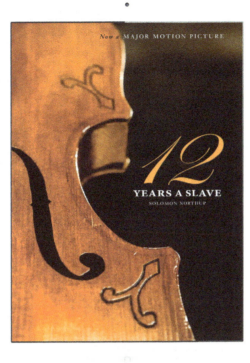
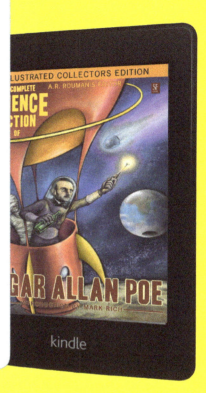
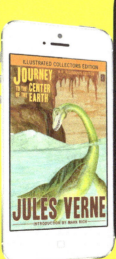
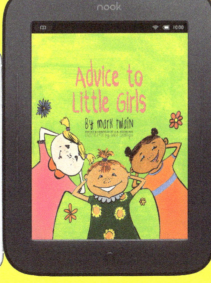

BUILD A CLASSIC LIBRARY FOR YOUR KIDS
WWW.ADCLASSICBOOKS.COM
The greats from the past two thousand years

CPSIA information can be obtained
at www.ICGtesting.com
Printed in the USA
LVHW07s0734240418
574630LV00031B/419/P